A 2 K C

ABLE TO KILL CAIN

Franklin A. McLeoud II

ARCHWAY
PUBLISHING

This book is a work of non-fiction. Unless otherwise noted, the author and the publisher
make no explicit guarantees as to the accuracy of the information contained in this book and
in some cases, names of people and places have been altered to protect their privacy.

Archway Publishing books may be ordered through booksellers or by contacting:

Archway Publishing
1663 Liberty Drive
Bloomington, IN 47403
www.archwaypublishing.com
844-669-3957

Scripture quotations are from the Holy Bible, King James Version (Authorized Version). First published
in 1611. Quoted from the KJV Classic Reference Bible, Copyright © 1983 by The Zondervan Corporation.

ISBN: 978-1-6657-3740-1 (sc)
ISBN: 978-1-6657-3741-8 (e)

Library of Congress Control Number: 2023901069

Print information available on the last page.

Archway Publishing rev. date: 2/3/2023

DEDICATED TO: THE MCLEOUD AND FLETHER FAMILY
1/19/2013

"...it was the footprints I saw along the my journey.. the moments of dark despair.. the rainbow after the rain. Finally, it was that faint whisper, an invitation to a mountain that lead me to my Burning Bush! I was forced to take note of every single moment while deserted by reality and standing on Holy Ground. I didn't want to lose this opportunity to understand my becoming and purpose! The Supreme Ruler and Creator of Creation, right here, in my living room!"

CONTENTS

A2KC INTRODUCTION

The spring of 2013 brought more pain into my life than I could hardly imagine! I had just re-devoted my life back to Christ and opened my heart to loved ones who I had wronged in the past! Some of these situations where events that were brought upon me and others I took complete blame for! Before I forgave these individuals, I had to first learn how to forgive myself. This wasn't an easy task! My health was at a detrimental state where I could not work any longer and at this point, I had thrown in the towel!

Normal task became a full-time commitment like I was an hourly employee on my own clock! The enemy was hot on my trail! I had even convinced others that my end was drawing near. My mother became comfortable talking to me about empty lots in graveyards where my grandmother was laying at rest. Options of life insurance so the burden of my passing would be an easy task were also apart of everyday conversation. I hated who I was and regretted all of the decisions that I made that lead me to this point. Even then, I had no plans of giving victory to the grave just yet!

A sibling of mine came to my aid by moving into my neglected apartment. He and I had not seen eye to eye for years and I thought this would be the perfect opportunity to mend our relationship. We were your modern day Cain and Able! In my mind, our situations were reversed him being the older brother and I his junior. I asked GOD to help me heal our hearts and fix what was broken between us. This journey became a testimony and the birth canal to this very book! I had some work to do! The following years were full of trial and tribulation. There was so much going on in the world where every negative moment in the news became part of everyday life. People were so use to pain that showing it on TV became a spectacle rather than an opportunity for change. The more pain I witnessed around me, the more I became inspired to make that change! A2kC deals with enabling the disabled mind through sermons of healing and inspiration. Rather than Able returning from the dead to seek revenge on his brother, this book focuses on killing off Cain mentalities that disable us in life! Some aspects are addictions, setbacks, family curses, envy, jealousy, greed and anything that separates us from the LOVE OF GOD! We are not slaves to our circumstances nor victims to our mishaps! We are heroes of our own history and believers of a Faith which will drive us to Heaven! A Place where it all began! A place where there will be no more tears of sorrow nor evidence of pain! A place where shadows have no residence and victory will forever be our story!

Ask yourself, how much is your soul worth when gambling with an enemy who doesn't sleep nor slumbers? How much more time will you spend lost, wondering in circles to find your way? You have put so much on the line during your lifetime disabling your vision and condition. Your dreams have been shattered and your heart has been broken! Happiness has found a way to evict itself from your soul and has wondered into the lives of everybody else but yours. Your hope has been hung upside down and your  cup has been empty for years! It is time to put an expiration date on all of your worry and fear. Cain has made his way into your life to bleed you of your joy and you will now seek vengeance on everything that was taken from you! Like Job, you will receive double for your trouble and everyone who told you to curse GOD, will see his face through your deliverance! The enemy has set aside a special plan to capture your soul! Not only does he desire to hold it in captivity, but he is certain that you belong to him and will use it as a trophy! He wants to hang it on his fireplace to reflect on his never ending desire to become greater than our Father! He is even willing to put up a fight with the great Archangel Michael in hopes to win you over even in death like he did over Moses! We are children of GOD and he has made his declaration over our lives. That means, no matter how many times you have messed up, no matter how many times we have turned our backs on Him, no matter the situation, the battle belongs to our Lord and Savior, Jesus Christ!

This war has become more than just a battle for souls! It has become a laughing game to the enemy and I feel it is time to silence the clown! The time has come for an end to Policed crimes. We will not cry any longer over bodies slain for unjust reasons! No longer will we hold the hands of our oppressors and trust them to lead us out of bondage. You are Able to kill Cain and with the right tools, you can get away with it! If GOD be for you, than who can be against you!

PRAYER

In my darkest night be a light unto my path. In moments when I feel lost without any direction, be my compass along the way. When I have lost my love for others remind me of your sacrifice for what you did on the cross. Favor me when I am in need. Send your protectors when I am faced by evil GOD, when I have done wrong, forgive me for it is your face that ultimately desire to see. Thank you for being a burden barrier thank you for life, and most of all thank you for Salvation. It is your heavenly name that I call upon to make the worry go away. These & other blessings I beseech of you father!... Amen!!!

Jan. 19th 2013

It's actually 15 min till the 19th but I decided to get a head start. Have you ever been chased trying to run away from something horrible! When you finally catch your breath realizing that what targets you is not far behind! Panic seems inevitable and worry is following right behind. I believe the devil wants somethings I have! Something that GOD special-delivered to my door! Relentless is the enemy who knows your weakness, but power is a gift of someone who gives you strength!!

Jan. 22nd 2013

I spent the entire weekend in the house moping a lot my strange peculiar auditions with the Voice! It didn't work out in my favor but what happens to me afterwards is horrifying! Especially when I know that I have GOD given talent & you tell me otherwise! Maybe I'm using it for the wrong reason maybe there is another route or just maybe I'm not ready, I've been losing some of my faith lately & I don't/can't lose anymore. I need strength/Sampson even super humans face great responsibility when blessed with such power... I'm ready to ascend...

Feb. Is the yearly Start!

I slept so well last night because I fed my flesh which I've been losing sleep. I don't think that was the reason why I slept well but it did ease my mind. I feel so responsible lately that I feel so worked like a slave. Now I want peace more that I care about nutrition. (Missing meals) The conversation with what I fight is an ongoing war! How do I fight an enemy who knows my every weakness! Don't get into the Ring the battle is not yours!

Jan 28th 2013

My words are so distorted right now that I cannot even find a starting point.
I made a mistake, one of many that I truly regret. My covenant with GOD was
broken by me entering my flesh! It got the best of me & now I worry of my
consequences. The???

ABLES ADDRESS TO THE CHILDREN OF ZION

The night had brought so much rain that I was in and out of sleep. I was stuck in the back barn after gathering the last of the sheep and was applauded by the sound of thunder. Time was lost by staring at the long distance back to the house. Held captive by the storm I became nosey in my own shelter. Somehow, I began to find old objects that I thought were lost. Memory lane was the next mission when I found high school memorabilia in an old box. I had so much fun in the rain, that I almost wanted to move in, bedroom and all! My phone had enough energy to start a music phase which ultimately made me wander even more. After a while the rain stopped, and I made my way out of my prison. The morning brought so much joy as the sun danced in my room filling the quiet space with rays of love. Just over the hill, I heard someone yelling "Hurry! We are going to be late!! For some apparent reason, I was filled with so much strength. I felt like running! I felt like shouting just as loud as this peculiar fellow running for his life. I didn't even know this man but I felt kin to his journey. We started off jogging then we both picked up incredible speed just around the corner of my house. "We have to hurry, I don't want to miss the entrance," my friend uttered! His voice was full of assurance and obedience at the same time. "Grab ahold of my hand Adamson. The wind will carry us the rest of the way." Suddenly....my feet became light as paper and I found myself, for the first time, flying! This experience was just as I expected it to be. I had dreams before of my flight toward the heavens. Sometimes the dreams had missions, where I saved the planet. Other dreams allowed me to live in the sky where me and God had our most private moments. When it was time to land, I circled around the island a few more times. "Adamson," my companion shouted, "you'll need to hide in my coat." I became confused and asked my friend a series of questions. More importantly I wanted to know why I couldn't witness the event at hand. "The host are dressed in a light that would blind a weak eye. Their wings are used to cool the earth with the four winds. Watch, as the water obeys their feet." We made camp at the crest of a mountain where the sun seemed to get brighter and brighter. All the fish of the sea flew underwater in a circular motion and the birds of the sky followed in harmony. A great horn filled the lungs of the sky and two more followed in unison. "On your knees Adamson." My knees gave into his command weak as if my body knew what to do. I fell on my face and the most amazing devotion of songs of praise. Singing, "Hail The Almighty, "The King of Glory, Jehovah, our GOD!" Fire turned the heavens a bright red and The Mighty Throne appeared. "To gaze into HIS GLORY is the most amazing feeling. It is completion, embraceful, and fear in the most engaging manner." My friend was caught in a trance as a moth to a flame. At first glance when I looked at my travel agent, I thought I saw a golden hedge radiating above his head. His coat fell to the ground and what my eyes witnessed next was nothing short of a miracle. Armoured with four wings on the left and four on the right. From head to toe, a bright white fire burned all around him and I became afraid. The celestial creature flew off and joined a wave of heavenly host who were descending from above. When the angel left, I was still in shock neglecting the burning sensation from the light on my skin. Filled with even more fear, my strength left me and I noticed my garments were burning. While on the ground I was able to take a second glance at the heavenly throne. This time, the right seat was empty. Instantly the fire around me was no longer hot. I began to praise He who had come to my rescue. His eyes were penetrating right through me as if he knew already who I was. I felt warm inside, like the day before Christmas. Filled with the Holy Spirit, I became anxious to know him by name. His skin shined like the finest brass and his eyes were filled with the same fire that took over the angels' presence. A royal crown rested upon his head and the glory of God shined all around him. "Rise, for I am He who knew you before you were formed in the womb. I am King of all the heavenly hosts and I have come to your rescue." His voice was as a thunderous roar from a lion. I regained my strength after his command and rose to my feet. How could such a great King come to my aid? How could he recognize me in my moment of despair? Such a man had to be the most Holy of all creation.

In this sacred moment, there were no shadows nor shade from the light. It seemed that my own shadow had forsaken me as if it never existed. The ocean was calm even though there were multitudes of angels occupying the space using it as a sanctuary. Smiling, amazed at this spectacle, I wanted to join to see if I could do the same. There were many church services that I was apart of full of devotion and the most amazing choirs. This meeting reminded me of many revivals that I also attended where the message delivered was the anchor of my faith. I turned toward the throne and my Savior who rescued me from my fear had suddenly occupied the empty seat from above. My fear never returned because I knew in my heart that I was chosen to be at this place of divine intervention. His presence was still with me. The aroma of fresh flowers kept me company as the service went on. Suddenly, without a gray cloud in the sky, lightning flashed through the sky as a great archangel made his way toward what seemed to be an alter. He bowed in front of the throne in the most formal manner, then turned toward the host who waited patiently as an army anticipating a speech from a general. The mountain trembled as he began to speak. "Children of our King, I bring you the son of Adam and Eve, Able!" The host applauded as Able made his way toward the podium. He was clothed in a garment that was different from the rest of the angels. His halo was wrapped around his forehead with matching bracelets around his wrist. There was some writing bound on the jewelry in some language that I could not recognize. His eyes were shinning like two diamonds sparkling with a glow illuminated from the light. I almost wanted to cry at his beauty but I held my tears in exchange for the excitement which had tickled my belly. He stood boldly in front of the crowd as the pastor of the congregation and made his address. "We praise thee, O God, maker of Heaven and Earth, ruler over all dominion. To our Champion and King of Glory, Jesus! You are the example of the Love of which we will protect forever more. Honor and praise to our Mother, the Holy Spirit! For She has brought peace and comfort to us all. Our existence depends on you, Holy Trinity, for we are forever in your debt. Finally, to you, my family, host of the most high. You are guardians of the light and ambassadors of the Golden City! Thank you for accepting me at such a young age. Heaven has been my home for what seems only a short while now and I cannot wait for eternity. I come forth today to bring you a message of responsibility at which we are to deliver to the children of Zion. Man has once again found a way to turn toward the calamity of our enemy. As the third who was stricken from grace, we must now declare war on their oppressors. For they have declared war on us and our Father. The have poisoned the land with fear and destruction. They take food from the poor and leave crumbs of despair behind. How long have we engaged in battle against the serpent of hatred and confusion. We are mighty and the time has come to take immediate action toward our victory. Our brother, Michael, carries the heavy chain which will bind our adversary for a short while. Before the giant is slain, we will meet them at their camp and strike a blow that they will not recuperate from. We will flood their cities and bring forth a wrath this side of heaven will take delight in witnessing. Cain has infected the lives of the humans who seek entrance into our gates. We out number them by great numbers and there is no way to avoid their demise. Oh how my brother seeks even in this day, to take the lives of the worshipers. He has disabled their ability to have faith in all that we stand for. Drugs, violence, witchcraft, adultery, fornication, deceitfulness, backsliding, lasciviousness, killing, blasphemy and all kinds of sin at which we never have tasted. I have not come to take revenge on Cain nor do I wish his fate to hell. But I have come to kill off the mentality and wicked ways which aided my brother in my physical death.

Since the beginning of time, we have walked among the population of earth in secrecy. Our identity has been kept private as our Father has commanded us not to interfere with their decisions. He has also in the same breath commanded us to watch over his children and guide them away from darkness. The final war is approaching and our blades have been hungry for vengeance. Innocent lives have been taken in the name of justice and now we will fight on their behalf. Terrorist have invaded the homeland for retribution honoring their false gods. The tyrants of their land have made themselves rich with greed. Furthermore, the righteous no longer pray for peace and fear now spreads over the land like a disease. The very breath they borrow is a gift at which they take for granted. Man made materials are worshiped as if time will not make waste of them. The dragon has deceived them by imitating his former image before the Lord had cast him from heaven. We now descend upon him

and his followers to take back Eden. The sun shines as evidence of our living, for when he gave his spirit into the hands of the Father, it lost the will to bring forth the day. This is the very reason why we will never see evening in heaven. At dawn, the sun will cleanse the earth of darkness for the last time. The dining halls of our great kingdom await our tales of victory over darkness. Go now and dwell among them! Reveal yourselves to them in hope that they will turn from their wicked ways. Salute your horns as we prepare to gather the children of Zion both sleeping and non-sleeping. We will ride toward our victory on the backs of our white horses now roaming in Heaven. Peace be unto us all!" The congregation then turned toward the mountain and my entire body prickled with goosebumps. I instantly woke up in my room anxious to tell the world of this great sermon I was honored to be apart of.

CAUGHT UP /
THE VISITORS

I was alone to myself just a-minding my business, and GOD came to me announced his presence! Suddenly, I was taken away, caught by the spirit. My face hit the floor and my breath left my body as if I were slammed by a giant. Everything around me was harmony. I could hear the birds singing right outside my window. The noise from the bumble bees were loud in my ear as well as they robbed the flowers of their honey. It all had meaning as GOD intended this visit to be. This meeting had purpose and I could not be distracted. I was being invited to the table of the Most High. His voice perfumed my room saying, Adamson, who I have given favor must know where it came from. I AM GOD, the first and the last, the beginning and the end, Alpha and Omega. Why do you seek what has already been found? Reach toward Heaven, and the answers of my glory will be revealed to you." I felt as if I was watching a chord lit by a match headed toward an explosive moment that I wasn't prepared to handle. He continued. "The demonstration of love can be found in the ones around you. On this day, examine your family which I ultimately desire in heaven. It was my purpose in creation. Why do I love you so much? Why were you created to live among men to stand before me in trial after death? How do you survive even when you seem to serve my adversary? Because you were made from me. Because you are my family. Because you are a chosen vessel! Just like the angels in heaven who have never tasted the nectar of sin, you remain kin to the many who stayed after the fallen few." The more I heard his voice, the more I became convinced that my heredity had more than a royal meaning. It was divine! "A mother who bares the child, never forsakes the path of giving birth. Even when the child sits on death row, she will say to herself that her child is honest and full of truth. She loves regardless, right or wrong that which is her own. This is the example of true love." God wanted to reveal himself to me as a caring Father in a way as the Holy Spirit encountered that night with Mary. He loves me because I am in Him. The son of Creation conceived by divine will and purpose. We cannot choose our parents but our parents have a part on choosing us! Everything started to make sense to me. There were so many times I had been rescued from death. So much that I had to be thankful for. I began to reminisce on the many times I was faced with favor instead of fate. I wanted shout with praise but my lips remained shut for the Lord was not done with me yet. This knowledge came with a price. Just when the Father gave me his will with heavy chastising manner, the holy spirit came to comfort me right behind Him. "Know this! What your Father has revealed to you is all out of Love. He cares for you so much that he was willing to offer you something valuable. Knowledge is power Adamson. So now that you know, you cannot say that it was never told to you on the day of testimony. On this day, you must give an account of all that you have done on earth. Know that some were born to serve Love, but you were created to demonstrate Love as Jesus did! His disciples were servants of Love but after his ascension, they became demonstrators of Love! Through this act, your Father can see through your earthly eyes. He gets to reveal himself to those who wish to follow him! It is your responsibility to guide them toward the light when they are lost in sin. There is so much that he can do! Why not join him and become witnesses of his true power? The war has already been won. On this day I made the decision to rededicate myself to the winning team!

"I KILLED A MAN!"

We all have to face our hidden sin, but can all sin be forgiven? Moses killed a man but was hand delivered to Heaven! Solomon had many wives but was highly favored by GOD. Peter promised Jesus that he would follow Him even until death and ended up denying him three times. GOD knew us before we knew ourselves. He even knew the sins we commit before they are done. Je justified his love for us by choosing us anyway. Paul says that he does not treat us as our sins deserve. There is no sin greater than the next. Sin is sin. It separates us from his love and dims our our chance at salvation. Everything happens when you find your purpose and nothing happens until you do. Can you tell me of any sin that has been committed that GOD hasn't thought of? Let's dig deeper into what seemed to be the end of the story of Moses. In Jude, the writer tells us that GOD sent his arch-angel to retrieve the body of Moses. On his way to do what was commanded of him, the devil came to put up a fight for the corpse. How could the devil challenge a great angel over a shell? What did he want with the body of the man behind Egypt's first exodus? Pharoh's anger must have transferred into the devils mind. I believe that he thought that Moses had committed the ultimate sin by taking the life of a man. I also believe that since he is the ultimate deceiver, he wanted the body as a trophy for his followers. Could he have thought that his fight for Moses should deserve some reward? Could he actually think that GOD would trade his body for winning his soul? You think that you have it so bad, don't you? We should rejoice when the weight of the world gets heavy on our shoulders. The adversary desires you so much, that he is willing to contend against archangels for your body even when he has lost your soul. He wants your body to hang over his fireplace to gaze upon it in effort to satisfy his pride. Your task is heavy because you are chosen to lead a generation out of bondage. Just don't kill anyone on your journey!

LOST AND FOUND

Have you ever been looking for something that you gave up on? You may have thought to yourself that there is no way you will find this particular item ever again. I found myself wandering around my house for a couple of hours looking for a necklace that had a halo around a silver cross I bought years before I graduated from college. I must have went through every article of clothing I owned. There were suitcases, closets, bookbags, and even pantry closets emptied from my rage growing by the second. Before I knew it, my entire house looked like a wasteland of debri and I became comfortable laying on the mountains of clothes scattered throughout my home. I must have drifted off when the spirit began to talk to me. "What you search so hard for is not hard to find. Consider your home like the center of your heart. Cleanse your mind, body, and soul and you will find what you are after so diligently." It took me three days to clean my home. I took two more days to re-arrange my pantry. Finally, I finished my temple by folding and hanging all of my clothes. One particular Sunday, I pulled out some dress shoes that I hadn't worn in years. I pieced together the perfect outfit for this Easter Sunday and I had just the shoe to bring the outfit fully together. The outfit was laid out the night before but I left the shoes in the back of the closet. The next day I waited until I was dressed until I went and grabbed my shoes. I slipped on the left shoe with no problem. Then, I tried to slide in my right shoe and as soon as my foot reached the top of my shoe I felt something unfamiliar. I reached in and low and behold, there was that necklace I gave up on all along. I remembered what the Holy Spirit told me and instantly a voice from heaven caught my attention in a daydream. "Your life has been filled with so much debri even to the point where you have lost so much faith. You went looking for me and tore your life apart wandering where I was as if I had forsaken you. I admired your search so much that I sent you my Spirit to comfort you. When you obeyed, you allowed my Son to wash you in his blood. Significantly, you find me right where you left me. I never left you my child. Know this, that you can't wear me like a charm or necklace. I cannot be shown off to your friends when you want to be flashy. If you keep me inside your heart, you will always know that I'm always with you, even till the end of time!"

How many times have we talked about the love of God only when its convenient? How many crosses do we own that we wear but often forget the meaning behind it. GOD has never abandoned us only to be rediscovered when the moment was just right. Even though we think we can hide from him, in the back of our minds we know it is impossible to escape the Creator of the Universe! Cain found this out hiding from GOD in the Garden of Eden!

HEAVEN IS HIRING

My disease has finally gotten to the point where I could no longer work a normal 9-5 everyday. My diabetes acts up if I don't eat properly, or if I eat the things that I know I am not supposed to eat. Sending my sugar into orbit (if you know what I mean) over 300. Then the people on my job would be scared to death and panic and not know what to do, only to look in my phone and call my Mother who lives 2-hours away to tell them to call an ambulance to get me to Piedmont Hospital.

I have had several good jobs where I loved to go to work and perform at an amazing rate but, my disease would not allow me to stay and complete a normal day. I left for lunch one day to cross the road to only get ran over by a car. Boy I didn't see that car coming!!! I tried to go between two cars while they were sitting at the light and the light changed and I got hit. Now ya'll talking bout some pain- this added to my already existing diabetic disease. The ambulance rushed me to Grady Memorial hospital where it looked like I laid on a table with my leg open for 5-hours. They had to perform surgery and place a rod and screws in my leg. I had just landed a job with Fed-ex and I was doing my (thang) as the young people would say. While laying on that table with my leg open my Mother was already on the way to Atlanta to help my Uncle with a catering job he was doing for the school. She had to tell my Uncle that she would have to split her time between me and him. I got so furious!! I did not understand why my Mother had to leave me at my time of need. She told me that they had already been paid and to get her share of the money she had to do some of the work. I began to call on God after she left and told the Lord I needed a heavenly job because I didn't think I could endure any more upsets on this side and to just come and get me while I was on that table waiting for them to sew me up. While going in and out of consciousness I begin to ask God what was it he was trying to get me to do before I leave this earth? I had been doing some speaking but that was not my only calling, I also had been doing some singing but it was R&B and I know that was not my calling, and then he spoke to me and said the gift that is already within you- you need to perfect that. Work on the gift of music and writing. Why are you looking for something that will make you uncomfortable in your own skin? Do what already comes natural to you. As you already know I called my Mother after I was back in my room after surgery and asked her how much longer was it going to take her to finish up with my Uncle and she let me know she was already in the hospital on the way up to my room. I could not wait to share with her the message God had given me. Now I had to ask God to put my resume on hold because I wouldn't need to go to heaven to do that job right away. But Heaven is hiring willing workers to go into the highways and byways to compel men and women to come to him. Do you have your application in? If not what are you waiting on? There is plenty of work to be done in the vineyard.

THROWN INTO THE FURNACE

My, my, my, some of these trials bring some show nuff heat into my life. I believe I have been thrown into the furnace for a couple of reasons. 1- for a testimony. 2- to give God Glory, 3- to help somebody else thru the same trial that I went thru. I could go on but I did say a couple of reasons. Heat defines who you are. The longer you are in it, the more refined you will be. Or let's say the more you can take from your oppressors.

Sometimes it is so hot(the issue) I have to back-up and approach it again. Then I have to come in another way because the entrance was blocked from me taking so long. God allows some things to happen to us so he can get the Glory. Does that make sense? I am in the furnace now but, once I am refined as pure brass I can overcome the toughest steel from a sword or arrow or dart that the enemy throws at me. Am I invisible? No.

Am I invisible? No. Well what am I? I have been thrown into the furnace to be able to endure some more trials and tribulations to come in my life and to help those around me, to go thru with me to be able to understand that God was preparing me for something greater than even I didn't understand at the time. In other words he was building me up so I could withstand some heat. And now I really need to be able to grasp my mission and go on running full steam ahead. For now I see my time is near and I want to be able to leave proof behind me that my life was not in vain. You might not get this now but, as my Pastor Rev. Milton Hughes would say- you'll get it on the way home.

RECOGNIZING THE CALL

Do you know when God is calling you? How does he get your attention? How will you know if it is God? All these questions lead up to one answer. My sheep will hear my voice and will hearken unto me. I will come to them in visions and dreams. Many times we hear and choose to ignore him. But my call was so strange that I knew it had to be God calling me because I had never heard that voice before. It was so different from any voice I had ever heard in my life. When it happened I had no choice but to pay attention. I had been running for a very long time, and had I listened to my Mother I would have probably answered my call sooner. But these children today are quick to speak and slow to listen. We want it our way or no way. And I don't like to tell my Mother she was right but, ya'll she was!!! We grow and learn from our mistakes(some of us) and from then on we are careful not to repeat the same mistakes if possible. There is something about the way God calls you. And it is not like anything you have ever heard of. I really can not explain it. But I will say this! He had my attention and it didn't take me long to know who he was. The calling on my life he let me know had been wasted by me doing other things I should not have done. Sure I operated in my gift but, I could have been more productive had I obeyed earlier in life instead of waiting until it was almost over. That is why he said serve him in thy youth so as you get older, it won't be so hard to do. Now that I was in the eve of my life, time was running out and he had to share with me quickly what I had time left enough to do. And that was to warn my family that Hell and Heaven was real and to get themselves ready for the coming of the Lord. Please be ready to recognize the call.

HOW TO SURRENDER

Does anyone know how to surrender? I mean give yourself totally to God? Let go of all the controls you have on your life and allow God to do what he is suppose to do. My Mother plays a hymn entitled I Surrender All. (Commonly found in the Baptist Red Book). But it simply means my will is no longer present and I am giving myself to God to do the will of God. It also takes you thru giving up things that you thought you had to have and shows you that they weren't really as important as you thought them to be. It means accepting the perfect will of God and submitting to him. Not your way but his way. Not your will but his. When you do this you can hear, feel, and witness his amazing power in your life. But you already know God had to pay a price. And so do we in the form of our own cross. Remember Must Jesus bear the cross alone and all the world go free? No there's a cross for everyone and there's a cross for me. The consecrated cross I'll bear til death shall set me free? And then go home my crown to wear for there's a cross for me. But it starts on how to surrender.

GIANTS IN CANAAN

The Lord showed a giant to me one day that I thought I could not handle. When he showed him to me I was so small, but once I put my trust in him that giant had to fall. My situations were to me as giants, because they seemed to tall for me to handle. I would pray and ask God to take care of them, then I would find myself dipping into the situation myself and not trusting God and allowing him to handle it. I have been faced with some of the same giants more than once because I did not defeat them the first time. So after I am faced with the giant again, the second round would be just a little bit harder for him to fall. My giants were my own fault. Sometimes fear would set in and I would look at the giant instead of God. It's amazing how we can tackle some things, but when it appears that things are larger than they appear to be we panic. Well it is the same thing with giants. They may appear to be that tall but, God has a way of going ahead and preparing the battle for us to win. Giants do die. The bigger they are the harder they fall. And so it is with the giant situations in life. If we put our trust in God they too crumble and fall. Things seem so much easier when we are in the will of God. Even a giant!

DAY OF REDEMPTION II

I have discovered that there is no point hiding from God. There are also side effects to hiding as well. Cain killed his brother Abel and thought he could run from his sin. God knew what was going to happen even before it happened and banned Cain and his family from the garden of Eden. Cain thought that running from God would justify the incident. Day of Redemption II asking God for forgiveness again even when he has blessed you beyond your sin. Psalms 103 states that God does not treat us as our sin deserves. That means he constantly shows us favor (grace) even when we are wrong. He blessed me when I break my promises with him, not because I'm saved but, but because of his unconditional love.

HOW TO WASH YOUR ENEMIES FEET

Just as Jesus washed Judas's feet, he was showing us humility when dealing with the enemy. Now Jesus knew that Judas would be the one to betray him. But he still treated him as if he knew nothing. It is our flesh that the enemy seeks to devour once he is made aware of our destiny. (Just as he did Job) You can't get upset or attack a person if they do you wrong. It was not them per say- but the spirit within them that wronged you.

Remember when they were at the last supper Jesus said one of you will betray me. When they were in the Garden of Gethsemane Judas betrayed Jesus with a kiss. Sometimes you will have to do things you ordinarily would not do so God can get the glory. The enemy will be confused, but when you obey God he will take care of the enemy. Jesus allowed the spirit that controlled his body to receive the kiss of betrayal from Judas. But God meant for it to happen. We were fooled I know in the beginning. But everyone has to fight for the purpose which God orchestrates. Attack the spirit... not the person. You may allow some spirits to kiss you on the cheek... but know the Master will deliver you from all evil point blank!

WHY ARE YOU SO CLINGY
TO YOUR CROSS

Remember you must transition beyond your cross in order to see God! It is a process. SIN is so sweet in the beginning but so sour in the end. The memories of pain & not letting go of negativity makes you hold on to your cross more. How do you let go of it and move even further to crucifying yourself. Leaving pain to move toward greater pain can be inhumane and rough. Consider all things a test with a greater reward in the end.

Transitioning begins with letting go of pain and self actualization. Crucifying can and will be a journey. But if you start with God in the beginning... the end will be sweet. I'm not saying it won't be hard, but if you start right - then you will end up right.

THIS MEANS WAR!!

We are in a spiritual battle whether you know it or not. The devil against God. Good against evil. Sinners vs. Saints. Righteousness against wickedness. I could go on and on. But we are in a war. Christians will be on the battlefield until after the great tribulation. Satan and his demons are trying to conquer the world and take whomever he can with him to the lake of fire and brimstone. We have to fight this battle with the weapons that are not carnal. We have to put on the whole armour of God to fight in this war. In the Bible Ephesians Chapter 6:verse 11 - 18 tells us to put on the whole armour of God to be able to stand against the devil and demons. In order to fight this war you need your weapons to win. Don't go into war unprepared to fight. You will not win!! God has already given us the tools to win and if we follow his word we will be successful. This war is very serious. Your soul is at stake. Guard it with your life. Being prepared is half the battle. Learn your enemy and what he is capable of. Your soul depends on it. Declare war on the Enemy and prepare to be in the fight for your life.

NO MATTER HOW DARK IT MAY SEEM

There is a saying that the darkest hour is just before day. It's true. It seems that right before daylight it is very dark, or it takes forever for daybreak to come. But in this obstacle course of life you will encounter a lot of dark situations that will seem to have no light at the end of the tunnel. Light cannot take the place of darkness and neither darkness can take the place of light. So when we are going thru our dark periods it seems that the light will never come, or that it seems like forever to get

here. Light is when you can see everything all around you and you can accomplish many things. But in the darkness it's impossible to see your way as you could see in the light. When you are faced with dark days remember it can't last for long. The light has to take its place. Your dark days are but for a moment. The light will come and you can focus on even brighter days ahead. But we all must enjoy the light so we can appreciate the darkness. Remember it is only temporary, but necessary. So no matter how dark it may seem, there will be LIGHT!!!

WARNING-DO NOT PROCEED!!

There are some who will answer my call & there are others who will run away from it in fear. You who hear my voice are to prepare, and those do not will suffer. Sometimes, even on the path that I have laid aside for you, the enemy will cross your path to make you think that the road ahead is dangerous. The enemy will try and sell you another road map. (to throw you off track) What has happened is the road ahead is under construction and needs to be worked on.

There are alot of pot holes and they need to be filled. As of now do not proceed. God is providing you a safer way out! Caution is all around you and warning signs are up for you to see. Pay attention to the signs that are up everywhere to keep you safe from all hurt harm and danger. The enemy's job is to make you detour off the course that God has ordained you to stay on. If you see warning signs take caution - DO NOT PROCEED!!!

A LETTER TO MY MOTHER AND GRANDMOTHER

During my writing the Lord came to me to talk to my Mother-Anita Hill Griffin and my Grandmother Mary Fletcher. But I want to talk the Mothers' who have similar situations and have suffered the loss of a child or children. God has chosen you to have chosen children, & out of your womb God will show you how worthy he is. It doesn't make sense to you when God's plan is rough on your children. Your children will be crucified yet you have to watch them carry their own cross to Calvary. Children of God carry assignments that we as the Mothers' can not complete. Sometimes falling on your back

ANITA HILL & GRANDMOTHER MARY FLETCHER

looking death in the eyes. Sometimes stricken with a plague or even chosen to die. We need your help Mothers' to warn, protect, help us heal, provide shelter when needed, and give direction in the right way to go. We may need you to help us navigate a different direction to travel when we get stuck in the traffic of life. God will not send your children somewhere he or she has not been. He already has a ram in the bush. Just when God has you to commit them back to him- it just may be a test of your faith to see how much you love him. Anita you were allowed to see your Mothers' death happen before your very eyes to help you deal with your Grandmothers' and the death of your first born son (me). Remember death is the human sacrifice as a gateway to see God. He had to make you strong, then stronger to be able to handle what was to come years later on down the road. Ironic isn't it? The way God does things to prepare us is just amazing. Now who wouldn't serve a God like that!!!!

BURN THEM WITH FIRE

The wages of sin is death. But the gift of God is eternal life. That scripture is found in Romans 6:23 in the new testament. Their is a consequence for all those who do not repent of their sins and accept Jesus as their Lord and personal Savior.

When Lucifer was thrown out of Heaven he took 1/3 of the angels with him that are now demons. Their job is to keep us from accepting Jesus Christ and to keep our minds off of Jesus and to focus on what the world does which will not gain us any reward in Heaven. What profited a man to gain the whole world and to lose his own soul?(Mathew 16:26)

When the Righteous judge shall read to us what we did we do with the gifts and talents that were given to us and have we accepted Jesus Christ and have we repented of our sins and made him Lord of our lives? Then he will tell us to depart from him to the lake of fire and brimstone to burn for an eternity. It seems cruel and unusual right? But God said he is not a man that he should lie. So are you prepared to spend eternity burning? Or will you make the choice so you will be able to spend eternity with God. If you do not choose God you have really made your decision whether you know it or not. A song that my Mother sings when it is time for the invitation to discipleship is I've Decided to Make Jesus My Choice. I hear all the time that I don't wanna live in hell then die and go to hell. Being burnt by fire forever is not an option that I want to deal with. So choose you this day whom you will serve.

BOOT CAMP IN THE DESERT

So you asked what is Boot Camp? Well, it's sorta like training in the military where you do extensive training You are also preparing to be a soldier and get in shape to be able to fight off the enemy. So it in the army of the Lord. To be able to win against the enemy you have to train for it. Trust me you cannot go into a battle with satan unprepared. This war as I have said before is spiritual. Temptation is a trick, it aids the enemy by attacking your mind. The Devil does not have any new tricks. Just new ways to trick you. Since your mind is ongoing, why not cause a traffic jam. I keep telling you same devil same tricks. There is someone in Heaven that I want to see and I am not going to allow the devil to trick me out of my opportunity to see my loved ones who are in Heaven already enjoying Jesus. Training is vital and of the upmost importance. Graduate from Boot Camp and Basic Training in the Desert.

CHRISTIAN AFFAIR

How could I love you and open my heart to you when sin is my significant other? Is God mad at me? Is this the reason I suffer? These are questions I ask myself. What is a diamond without pressure? A cubic zirconia.

When you are tried it's like fire shaping steel or iron a precious metal so you can be the best you can be. Once the mold of you has been complete you have a cooling period where you are shaped into the you that God would have you to be. Iron sharpens iron. And when it is finished it becomes shiny and glossy and able to cut thru the thickest of materials. The relationship between you and God is just that!!! When sin is committed God cannot dwell in an unclean place. When sin comes in, your tabernacle is dirty and has to be cleansed. Mere soap and water will not wash away your sinful nature. What can wash away my sin? Nothing but the blood but of Jesus. What can make me whole again? Nothing but the blood of Jesus. Do not have an affair with sin. It only creates chaos. When you are in love with Jesus there is no room for the significant other which is sin. But the relationship you have with Jesus Christ will conquer all.

BLIND FAITH

Faith is the substance of things hoped for the evidence of things not seen. To be perfectly honest blind faith. It is the hope and prayer of whatever you are asking God to do for you and the belief that God will do it.

I must admit that I fall short in this area a lot of times because I have right now faith (most of us do). I want what I want right then and now. I am impatient when I have to wait for an answer from God or something from God. Is that right or fair? No. God does not answer in our time because he is not like man, or is he to be compared to him because his ways are not our ways and his thoughts are not our thoughts. We are made in his image but we don't have his judgement qualities. Nor his mercy or grace. He gives to who he wants and how he wants to. Whenever things don't happen when we want them to we have to exercise our faith to know God will do it whenever he desires to. Dottie Peoples has a song entitled He's an on Time God meaning whenever he does come, he's on time. Not by our time but by his. Friends that is Blind Faith!!!

CRUCIFY YOURSELF

There is a scripture in the Bible that tells us if we are to be followers of Christ we have to first have deny ourselves take up our cross and follow him. It sounds simple but is a day to day struggle. Some days are easier than others. And God did not say it was going to be easy. As a matter of fact he told us we would go thru trials and tribulations on this side. But if we endure until the end, the race would be given to us.

So to deny the things we want as to what we need can be hard. As a matter of fact I find myself listing the ones that are very hard and trying to handle them one at a time. So I can say I am doing better in this area of my life and need to keep pressing forward on the task at hand. I have several issues with my flesh, not submitting and bringing it under subjection, not to do my will but the will of God. It requires some fasting as well and turning down your plate. But with my disease I have to eat to live. So what I do is 30-minutes to an hour out of the day I fast on that particular issue that I am having trouble with. Then I repeat it for the next few days until I have a substantial amount of time built up. Sometimes I take away the tv (my eyesight is gone in one eye anyway) so that one is easy. I don't eat certain foods that I love(Mexican). I don't go to my favorite stores(mall). Things of this nature. It's hard but doable. You can crucify your flesh and in doing so you will find the things that you thought you wanted you really didn't need. But God does reward those that diligently seek him.

NAILS AND A CROSS

This life is filled with so many crosses to bear. If you pass one test then the next test is right around the corner. And definitely one cross differs from the other. One cross can be extremely heavy. The next cross can be very light. Sometimes the cross comes with nails, and then they can also come with screws with severe pain.

My cross seems to be heavy all the time because I worry from day to day about my illness. Sometimes losing a lot of sleep, and that causes my illness to act up as well because then I need medication for insomnia.

I am trying to learn how to not worry so much and let one day take care of itself, but this illness will not let up. I know I have to carry my cross wherever I go and am reminded that I am not perfect but, God's grace and mercy is always present to help me endure with this life's thorns. Most of the time I can feel a nail going in me. And then I can feel a nail being removed from me. I thank God for the ones that he removes from me and sometimes I don't even feel them when he takes them out. I find out when I return back to the Dr. and he says there has been no significant change or one of my organs has gotten stronger and the medication he prescribed for that organ is no longer needed. Then I breathe a SIGH OF RELIEF! BECAUSE! Then I know God has removed another nail from me and my worrying downgrades just a little bit.

These nails and a cross are always present and in this life you will have your own to bear. No one can bear them for you. There is a hymn my Mother plays from time to time.

Must Jesus bear the cross alone and all the world go free?
No there's a cross for everyone and there's a cross for me.

So true a song even to this very day. And remember no cross, no crown. Some of the nails you have in your cross are needed to keep your cross together. Some of them can be removed and be replaced by a different type. And then some can be removed all together. I am learning to be thank-full for my nails and my cross.

THE HUNGER! PART ONE

It came to pass that on this night the son of man would be tried with his loyalty by his Master. He had been given the simple duty of guarding the home while his Master was away. While the servant stays on guard he dresses in the garment of mercy and tries on the helmet of knowledge. All items which are foreign to touch. He arrives home unexpectedly and now is in shame.

A new day arises and the decision has been made since you were forbidden to touch certain items at the Masters' house and were so hungry and did not ask, for nourishment or substinance, you will be fed in increments only for survival and not for your health.

Wow, what a punishment that was given from the Master of the house. Instead of being able to eat whenever he wanted to he had to be fed whenever the Master told someone to feed him. How inconvenient for the servant, so now his overall health was in jeopardy because of his disobedience. So it pays to obey them that have the rule over you in all things, because disobedience like sin has a consequence.

KILLING THE ADDICTION: (FEATURING MARY MAGDALENE)

How do you deal with an addiction? Well let's look at a situation I have been dealing with for quite sometime. We all have issues with our flesh. We might not admit it to others but, if we are honest with ourselves we all have some type of addiction whether we want to own up to it or not. Some of our issues are harder to submit to the spirit than others. It is a daily struggle to sometimes to want to submit. But we have to pray and seek Gods' face on these matters and fast (for those of us who can) for that particular matter. Killing an addiction is hard but, with Gods' help it can be done. One of my favorite characters in the bible was Mary Magdalene who was caught in the very act of adultery. From the looks of it she had been dealing with this issue for quite some time and had not conquered it. Only when she was about to be stoned for her offense did Jesus step in and ask her where her accusers were and did

any man accuse her and she told the Lord no, then he replied neither did he and told her to go and sin no more. She took that opportunity to take her addiction and kill it.

She was obedient to the Lord and for that reason he forgave her and she had a brand new start.

Sometimes we don't get those chances to start all over. But God has Mercy on us and allows us time to get it right. For us that get those 2nd chances we should seize the moment to kill whatever addiction that is holding us back from entering the kingdom of heaven. Repent is for every man woman boy or girl who believes that God will forgive you and you can kill whatever addiction you have to kill.

HOW TO WALK ON WATER

This point in my life was my faith being tested. Just like when Jesus asked Peter to come out on the water, he was testing Peter to do the impossible and put his faith into action. Remember faith without works is dead.

So at this point in my life with all my failing organs happening to me one after the other. My faith was being tested as well as my belief in God to do the impossible in my body. I know that God is real and I had to find out for myself how to lean and depend on God for everything in my life from now on. Yes I called my Mother again because whenever I was in doubt, she would direct me to the word of God for the answer that I would need and be able to apply it to this very aspect of my life. Of course she directed me to the story in the bible where Peter was asked to trust Jesus and come to him out on the water. He had to forget about everything around him and concentrate on Jesus. When he did this he was walking on water but, when he took his eyes off Jesus he began to sink. Isn't that what happens to us when we allow things and people to distract us and the situation we are in begins to consume us totally until we cry out for Jesus to save us from that situation. I found out I could walk on any type of water when I had my eyes on Jesus. When I allowed my attention to be taken off Jesus, all kinds of distractions were able to keep me in sinking water where I was about to drown. But when I realized (came to myself) in every situation God told me to acknowledge him and he would direct my path, I was able to so more than walk on the water. I could glide, skate, run, jump, and lay on top of the water and not worry about drowning. Halelujah! To the Lamb of God. I looked at my disease thru a different set of eyes.

Whenever death was gonna come I wasn't worried about it anymore. My disease didn't have me bound any longer. I finally gave it to Jesus and was not in fear of dying any more. Now I welcomed death with a different outlook. And knew my body was just the stage where it had to take place. I knew for me to die was inevitable but, Christ I would gain. My Mother helped to see me conquering the water was just another cross I had to carry to a certain point and get ready for the next task at hand. I learned late but, I liked the fact that I could walk on water.

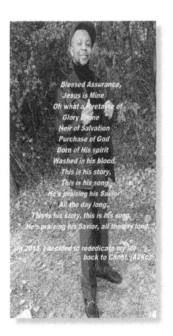

FRANKLIN POSING OUTSIDE OF CHURCH. THESE WORDS TO
HIS FAVORITE HYMN WERE IN HIS OBITUARY.

A2KC - CANCELING
FUNERAL ARRANGEMENTS

Today I went to the Dr. and was given more disappointing news about my diabetic disease and what to expect next as I try to live from day to day. I called my Mother as always to give her the report as to how to go about this next phase with the treatment and medication dosage. She always had encouraging words and prayed about whatever the Dr. told me and we looked at options and how to include another medication to my list.

I began to tell her I am so tired of taking medicine and that I was ready to give up. She went into her normal sermon of if I stop fighting what would she be left to do routine. Then she would say as long as you fight I'll help you fight! But it is not going to be easy. You have to wanna live and not die. I would say you don't know what it is like to get up every morning taking medicine and all thru the day, then watching what I eat and how much to eat, then going to the bathroom shortly after to dispose of all I had eaten and not regaining my weight. It was so depressing that I would get quiet and just stay in my room and not want to talk to anyone.

I began to think about death alot more and how easy it would be to just say the heck with all of this and check out of this life and be done with everything: the pain, the medicine, the Dr.'s, the back and forth to appointments, changing medication, just all of it. I wanted this life to be over with and not deal with nothing.

My Mother began to minister to me in a way that I had never heard her before, she told me how to speak life and not death and that life and death was in the power of the tongue. And then she told me to start speaking those things that be not as tho they were. In spite of this progressing disease, I yet had the power with God to overcome it. I did not have to give in to the thoughts of suicide because of on going issues. Everyday was not going to be a bed of roses and that I was going to be stuck by thorns every now and then. And when it happens just treat the wound and make sure it does not get infected or get worse. Then she reminded me of our Lord and Saviour Jesus Christ. How he knew the task that was before him and how he asked the Father to let this cup pass from him if it was his will.

The Lord did not opt out to end his life, instead he pressed forward to complete the mission that he was given. Instead he knew that death would come and he had to prepare to deal with the sins of the whole world and get ready to die for humanity. Wow! I then looked at my life in a totally different way. I had been planning my funeral and was not being fair to myself. Thank-you God for dying on the cross for my sins and giving me another chance to the right of the tree of life. I am canceling my funeral arrangements and I am going to live one day at a time.

STANDING AT THE BURNING BUSH

When I think about when I was diagnosed with type 1 diabetes (very abnormal) where the body makes no insulin at all, I have to admit that I did not take this as serious as I should have at the age of 18. My Mother thought she had done something wrong because she was asking the Dr. how I had it and she didn't. It was almost as if she was trying to take the disease from me to keep me from being sick. Now early on I still ate whatever I wanted and how much I wanted and never thought about counting carbs and sugars (so very important). I just kept on my destructive path to harming myself and not realizing it. However it did catch up with me eventually, and by then it was too late. I have to now take shots 4-times a day with meals to regulate my diabetes and keep my body on the right path. But if ignored it can lead to all types of organ dysfunctions which is what's happening to me now. I have to admit that I was trying to cheat and get by with what I wanted to eat but, it begin to tell on me because my glucose numbers were out of control. So now I am forced to watch and count everything I put in my mouth. I feel like I am being tested in more ways than one to get this disease under control. My burning bush was me also standing on a ground that was too hot for me to be on at that particular time. Before me now was God telling me to get ready for the next phase of trials that were to come in my life and to surrender to his will so I would be able to complete the task that he had for me to do. Yeah in the beginning I was reluctant to step out there and trust him but, as he was dealing with me, he eased my fear of what was coming and I began to take baby steps towards my mission. What he informed me of was so hot to the touch that I actually had in my physical body a slight temperature that I could not explain to my Mother. So I called her to come and take my temp and she informed me that I did have a slight fever. But I couldn't explain it. She began to treat me for the fever and I began to cool down within the hour. But now that I knew my mission, I was trying to handle it without going crazy. God called out to me and said "Franklin listen to me: (this ground where you are standing is the front of your blessing and at the end of the blessing will be me.) Just follow me and your reward will be given to you at the end. But you have got to be strong and make it. All kinds of things are going to happen to you but, the crown of life is still attainable if you persist. I know the ground around you is hot but, after our encounter is over you will be normal. Don't take this lightly and proceed with caution.

This burning bush is a warning from me to you to let you know some of the things you will go thru you will not understand now. But in the days to come I will come again to you not in this form but another way and in your dreams and reveal what is next. I had to get your attention and if you notice the bush is not consumed nor burned. This will not burn you but it may consume you physically. But know this: your soul belongs to me and cannot be burned or consumed if you continue to walk with me and let me guide you thru this life. You will see when you get to the other side what I mean if you hold out til the end.)

SHOWDOWN AT SUNDOWN

Do you not know that the devil is trying to get as many souls as he can before his time is up? The bible tell us to work while it is day because when the night cometh, no man can work. So you need to do all you can while you can when the sun is up. He has tried to get me so many times I can't even count them on my two hands. I know why the devil was after me and he let it be known he was not going to give up. I began my healing at my apartment in Sandy Springs and during this process my younger brother needed a place to stay after thanksgiving after living down in Dublin Ga. with my Mother. So me being the bigger brother I allowed him to come and stay with me. My baby brother was having trouble in school and so I put him in Job Corps in Albany Ga. where my Mothers' baby brother (uncle David) was over the Food Service Manager. Anyway I had enough to keep me busy with both of my brothers staying with me and present situation of healing from being hit by the car. I knew Satan was after me and it was a daily task to keep him away from me. I knew my soul was at risk and temptations were coming at me right and left. I was giving in to my flesh and allowing myself the pleasures I knew were wrong. Every time I would fall I would feel guilty and call my -(yep ya'll know what I'm about to say) Mother. Well as always she had the right advice for me, whether I wanted to hear it or not. She reminded me that we are not perfect, and no one but God is. She told me that whenever I fall that God is just and ready to forgive me and to repent, get back up, and try it again. I don't have to woller and remain in my sins and feel guilty for a long time. Get up and shake the dust off your feet and as my Grandmother

FRANKLIN A. MCLEOUD II

Mary would say-keep it moving. Don't let the devil come to the showdown at sundown to win. Get prepared and get ready for the fight of your life. Don't go to the showdown at sundown without your armour. Put on the whole armour of God and be ready to stand against the wiles of the devil, and having done all to stand, stand with the blessed assurance that you will win the battle if you run and faint not, your soul belongs to God. Protect it.

SEND IN THE WOLVES

We encounter traitors in life for all types of reasons. My Judas so to speak came in many different people who I thought were my friends and I had to learn the hard way who was genuine and was fake. I gave away money, clothes, shoes, cologne, and food. Now some of these people I knew not to deal with because my Mother had forewarned me but, as she would say you don't believe poop smells unless you step in it.

And so I had to find out the hard way. I lost who I thought were my closest friends only to find out they were using me only for what they could get out of me. I was allowing my kindness to be taken for weakness and being betrayed all at the same time. I would feed the wolves and they would go out and recruit more wolves because they heard the food I was preparing was good and they didn't have to contribute to eat. I was on a fixed income and my money would run out before the end of the month and then I would have to call my Mother to bail me out (as always) to bail me out until my check comes again. I also had to endure a 30-minute speech about my finances and money management for the rest of the month and had to repay whatever I borrowed. Sometimes whatever I borrowed took away from my monthly expenses only to borrow from my Mother again. These traitors are costing me money and when I go to them to ask for it back guess what? Yep you're right, they don't have it.

Judas betrayed Jesus for thirty pieces of silver. Was it worth it? Was it worth all that he encountered afterwards, then suicide? I had to quickly take an assessment of my true friends. Those I knew I could count on, and those who I knew would betray me in my time of need. Watch out! These wolves eat anything and everything and stop at nothing until it is all gone. Be careful who you allow into your inner most circle. And remember wolves travel in packs!!!!

FRANKLIN AND MOTHER - ANITA HIL

THE AUTHOR OF A2KC
FRANKLIN ANDRE DWAYNE MCLEOUD

FRANKLIN WITH HIS GODMOTHER - SONJA FLETCHER AND MOTHER - ANITA HILL

FRANKLIN GRADUATING WITH AN ASSOCIATES DEGREE IN MEDICAL SCIENCE.

FRANKLIN FEELING GOOD AFTER WASHING HIS MOTHER'S CAR

FRANKLIN A. MCLEOUD II